AI-Enabled Emergency Response

Enhancing Preparedness and Recovery Efforts

Table of Contents

Chapter 1. Introduction

Our special report dives into an essential, yet intriguing technological narrative – "AI-Enabled Emergency Response: Enhancing Preparedness and Recovery Efforts". Rather than daunting technobabble, we demystify the world of artificial intelligence, taking a comprehensive, down-to-earth approach to understand how this ever-evolving technology is quietly revolutionizing how we prepare for and recover from emergencies. We examine, in a language everyone can grasp, how emergency response teams utilize the power of AI to protect life, property, and environment more effectively than ever before. If you've ever longed to go beyond the headlines and truly comprehend the transformative potential of AI in a pivotal field like emergency management, this special report awaits you.

Chapter 2. Understanding Fundamentals of AI in Emergency Response

Artificial Intelligence– or AI – has steadily progressed from being a mere concept of science fiction to a powerful pragmatic tool used across a melange of sectors. Emergency response is one pivotal area where AI's potential is being harnessed to save lives, secure property, and prevent environmental devastation during times of crises. This chapter delves into the fundamentals of AI and its application to emergency response, rendering a clear picture of how this technology is facilitating our battle against disaster – be it natural or man-made.

2.1. Introduction to Artificial Intelligence

Artificial Intelligence utilizes machines and software to mimic cognitive functions that are typically associated with the human mind, such as understanding, reasoning, learning, and problem-solving. AI doesn't just operate uniquely; it is capable of refining its operations by 'learning' from its previous experiences or results, thus evolving over time.

A type of AI known as Machine Learning (ML) gives the system the ability to improve its performance without being explicitly programmed to do so. The system 'learns' through iteration, repeatedly modifying its processing to enhance the outcome based on the success of previous outcomes. This capacity to learn from experience allows AI systems to become more effective and efficient with each use.

2.2. AI in Emergency Response: An Overview

The application of AI in emergency response is a testament to the extent and reach of this technology. Emergency situations often manifest unpredictably, spanning from natural disasters such as floods, hurricanes, earthquakes, and wildfires, to human-made catastrophes, including industrial accidents, terrorist attacks, or critical health emergencies.

Historically, these situations have presented substantial challenges to responders due to their erratic nature. Human capacity to swiftly process copious amounts of data, predict outcomes, and make rapid decisions under intense pressure is limited. This is where AI steps in, bringing the power of rapid data processing, predictive modeling, and decision-making support to effectively respond to emergencies.

2.3. Rapid Data Processing

AI can process vast amounts of data swiftly and accurately. This ability is invaluable in emergency response, where every second counts, and resources must be allocated effectively and efficiently. Diverse data sources like meteorological reports, geographical data, social media, news feeds, and more are assessed in real-time, giving responders insights into the severity, location, and dimension of the disaster.

For instance, AI can analyze weather data to determine the likelihood of a flood, its potential magnitude, the regions that will likely be affected, and the optimal evacuation routes. It allows responders to make quick, informed decisions that could potentially save lives and minimize damage.

2.4. Predictive Modeling

Predictive modeling is a significant offshoot of AI and has been increasingly employed in emergency response initiatives. Using historical data and current inputs, AI systems can anticipate the future behavior or occurrence of events. For instance, AI can help predict where a wildfire might spread based on wind patterns, temperature, humidity, vegetation coverage, and terrain information.

Such predictions enable proactive measures – rather than reactive responses – ensuring better preparation and potentially lesser damage. These models also aid post-disaster recovery by providing insights into the areas that need the most immediate attention.

2.5. Decision-making Support

Decision-making during emergencies can be overwhelmingly taxing due to the sheer number and weight of variables at play. AI can significantly ease this burden by presenting data-driven insights and recommendations. From advice on the best allocation of resources to estimating the reach and impact of a disaster, AI tools can provide emergency management professionals with critical support.

AI can also simulate different response scenarios, allowing emergency planners to assess various strategies' effectiveness and anticipate possible outcomes. Such foresight can be crucial in deciding the best course of action under pressing circumstances.

2.6. Conclusion

AI's potential to improve emergency response is enormous. Its ability to analyze complex data, predict outcomes, and support decision-making processes has already proven significantly beneficial in rapidly evolving, high-stakes situations. As technology continues to evolve, we can expect AI's role in emergency response to expand and refine, making disaster management more effective than ever before.

The subsequent sections of this report will explore specific case studies showcasing AI's application in emergency response. We will delve into the intricacies of how AI has enabled responders to work more efficiently, effectively, and proactively in the face of emergencies – reaffirming our belief that AI is not a future prospect, but a practical reality shaping our world.

Chapter 3. Unveiling the Potential of Artificial Intelligence

Artificial intelligence is not merely another high-tech trend. It represents an evolving suite of technologies that embodies a powerful transformation for managing emergencies proficiently — a paradigm shift from traditional methods.

3.1. The Essence of AI

At its core, Artificial Intelligence, or AI, can be defined as a branch of computer science concerned with building machines capable of intelligent behavior. Rooted in complex algorithms and computational models, it uses vast data inputs to mimic several aspects of human intelligence, such as reasoning, learning, problem-solving, and perception.

From speech recognition systems like Siri and Alexa, to autonomous vehicles and predictive analytics, AI technologies permeate our daily lives, often in unseen ways. However, it's in the world of emergency management that these technologies have proven to be a real game-changer, pushing the boundaries of preparedness, response, and recovery to the next level.

3.2. Layers of Artificial Intelligence

AI isn't a monolithic entity; it boasts diverse subsets, including Machine Learning (ML), Natural Language Processing (NLP), Robotics and Computer Vision. Each has its unique role and application, yet, when combined, they constitute an effective tool of unprecedented potential.

1. **Machine Learning**: ML involves the development of algorithms that allow computers to learn from and make decisions or predictions based on data. This ability to "learn" from historical data underlies powerful predictive analytics in emergency management, forecasting potential disasters and crisis trends.

2. **Natural Language Processing**: NLP is all about communication; it enables machines to understand and interpret human language. Its applications range from sentiment analysis to real-time translation, aiding in efficient communication during a crisis.

3. **Robotics**: AI-powered robots can reach places where it's too dangerous for humans, rescuing victims, delivering aid, or assessing damage. Their utility shone during the Fukushima nuclear disaster, where robots were deployed to inspect and fix the reactor.

4. **Computer Vision**: CV involves machines gaining high-level understanding from digital images or videos. In emergency situations, this could mean using drone footage for damage assessment and survivor detection or interpreting satellite image data to anticipate a forest fire's path.

3.3. AI in Emergency Management: Prime Applications

A key charm of AI lies in its ability to be molded and adapted to suit a host of circumstances, making it a prime contender for application across various phases of emergency management.

1. **Prediction and Preparedness**: The heart of disaster management lies in how quickly and accurately potential threats can be foreseen. Machine Learning models can predict hurricanes, forest fires, or floods by analyzing historical weather data and tracking anomalies. This allows for more efficient

preparation, timely evacuation orders, and minimization of potential harm.

2. **During the Emergency**: AI's predictive capabilities extend to the disaster's ongoing phase as well. It can analyze data from sensors or social media to identify dangerous hotspots, track the disaster's progression and help responders navigate the affected area safely.

3. **Recovery and Rehabilitation**: Post-disaster, AI can assess infrastructural damage, identify victims in need of help, and help plan efficient rehabilitation strategies. By predicting future trends, it allows better planning to avoid or mitigate similar situations in the future.

3.4. AI in Emergency Management: Cutting-Edge Technology & Devices

Limitless possibilities open up with AI. Here are a few essential devices that are already enhancing our emergency management capabilities:

1. **Drones**: Whether it's delivering supplies, mapping wildfire progression, or conducting search and rescue operations, AI-enabled drones have emerged as versatile tools in crisis scenarios.

2. **Robotic Search & Rescue**: AI-supported robots can traverse disaster-stricken areas, conducting searches and rescues where human first responders may face unnecessary risk.

3. **Smart Sensors**: Invaluable during early warning or ongoing crises, AI-backed sensors can rapidly and accurately detect temperature changes, chemical leaks, or even changes in seismic activity.

4. **Remote Sensing Satellites**: These lucrative technologies can not only predict a myriad of disasters like storms or droughts but also

aid in managing them effectively. By constantly monitoring Earth's phenomena, these satellites can incorporate environmental data into AI models for precise predictions and mitigation strategies.

3.5. AI Limitations & Ethical Concerns

Despite its luminous promise, AI in emergency management isn't without challenges. Data accuracy and quality are critical for any effective AI system, and errors or biases in this foundational data can lead to flawed decisions and predictions. Furthermore, over-reliance on these technologies could lead to a reduced role for human intuition and expertise.

From a broader perspective, ethical concerns need addressing, such as who bears responsibility if an AI makes a wrong decision leading to harm, or privacy issues concerning the large-scale data collection AI often demands.

As the AI landscape continues to evolve, it is evident that its potential in emergency management is vast and largely unexplored. It can, and should, complement existing strategies, not replace them. The keys to unlocking this potential are persistent curiosity, groundbreaking innovation, and careful consideration of potential ethical challenges.

Chapter 4. Data Mining and Predictive Analysis: Anticipating Disasters

Disaster response efforts have drastically improved in recent decades, much of it due to advancements in data mining and predictive analysis. These areas of technological study have succeeded in more accurately forecasting natural disasters, helping to prepare communities for the worst and facilitating faster recovery times. This chapter will provide an overview of how data mining and predictive analysis function, and how these techniques are currently being applied in emergency management contexts.

4.1. What Are Data Mining and Predictive Analysis?

Data mining is a process that involves discovering patterns in large data sets, utilizing methods at the intersection of machine learning, statistics, and database systems. It is an essential method in artificial intelligence that extracts vital information from data, turning raw data into valuable insights.

Predictive analysis is a related field, employing statistics, modeling, machine learning, and artificial intelligence to sift through current and historical data to predict future events. It can be particularly helpful in predicting the occurrence, timing, and intensity of natural disasters.

4.2. Data Mining Process in Disaster Management

Data mining's role in disaster management involves processing vast volumes of data to yield relevant patterns and correlations. This process involves the following key steps:

1. Problem definition: The first step involves defining the specific goals of the data mining project, which can range from predicting cyclone paths to identifying communities most at risk in an earthquake.

2. Data selection: Data relevant to the defined problem is selected from a variety of sources including meteorological data, geological data, historical incident reports, and social media feeds.

3. Data cleaning: The collected data is then cleaned to rectify any errors and handle missing values to ensure accuracy in the patterns that will be subsequently detected.

4. Data transformation: The cleaned data is transformed into formats suitable for the mining process.

5. Data mining: Various techniques like clustering, classification, association, and regression are used to identify patterns and correlations in the structured data.

6. Interpretation and evaluation: The final step involves interpreting the discovered patterns and evaluating their usefulness in the context of emergency response.

4.3. Predictive Analysis for Disaster Anticipation

Predictive analysis uses myriad techniques to predict future disasters based on historical and real-time data. For instance, the occurrence of earthquakes and cyclones can be predicted by analyzing seismic and atmospheric data respectively. Furthermore, machine learning models can process variables such as past weather patterns, soil moistness levels, temperatures, and wind directions to predict the likelihood of forest fires.

The integration of AI with predictive analysis means that these models can learn from every disaster, refining their algorithms to improve the accuracy of predictions over time. The result is a powerful tool in disaster anticipation, allowing for preemptive measures to be put into place, which can significantly reduce the impact of such incidents.

4.4. Applications in Real-World Scenarios

AI-enabled data mining and predictive analysis have been applied to a variety of real-world scenarios:

1. Earthquake prediction: AI algorithms are being used to analyze seismic data to predict earthquakes. Sophisticated models have been developed that can recognize the subtle patterns in seismic waves, which often precede an earthquake.

2. Flood forecasting: Deep learning, a branch of AI, is being used to predict the severity and impact of flooding by analyzing weather data and geographical information. This enables authorities to organize evacuations and protect property against imminent flooding.

3. Wildfire detection: AI can analyze data from weather stations, satellites, and other relevant sources to predict the likelihood and spread of wildfires. This can help mobilize firefighters and evacuation plans more swiftly and accurately.

4.5. Future of Data Mining and Predictive Analysis

Looking to the future, it's clear that data mining and predictive analysis will play an increasingly crucial role in disaster management. As these tools become more refined, their predictions will become more accurate enabling more efficient and effective emergency responses.

Moreover, advancements in technologies, such as Internet of Things (IoT), can significantly improve data acquisition, providing more comprehensive and real-time data to feed into these AI algorithms.

With the ongoing development and integration of AI, data mining, and predictive analysis, the next generation of disaster management will see resources allocated more effectively, recovery efforts streamlined, and most crucially, lives saved.

In conclusion, data mining and predictive analysis have already begun revolutionizing emergency preparedness and recovery. As we continue to improve and refine these technologies, we only stand to benefit from a world more prepared for natural disasters and prepared to recover more quickly whenever they occur.

Chapter 5. AI in Action: Case Studies of AI-Powered Emergency Response

In the verdant heart of the Amazon, where wildfires have become a persistent menace, artificial intelligence is continuously learning and adapting, aiding in predicting the onset of emergent crises. A thousand miles away in San Francisco, an earthquake happens, and AI systems spring into action, guiding rescue teams and managing resources during these critical first moments. From the magnitude of natural disasters to the streets during rush-hour traffic, AI-enforced emergency response mechanisms are transforming the landscape at an increasing pace. Here we delve into detailed case studies of AI successfully enhancing emergency response capacity.

5.1. Predicting and Combatting Wildfires in the Amazon

The Amazon is the largest rainforest globally, representing over half of the world's remaining rainforests. Wildfires are a significant threat to this vital ecosystem, directly impacting biodiversity and global climate change patterns. A combination of predictive modeling, remote sensing via satellite imagery, and AI algorithms presents a highly integrated approach to curtail this issue.

This AI-system uses sensors to collect data from multiple sources, including weather conditions, forest density, and past fire patterns. The collated information is analyzed, and with machine learning algorithms, the system becomes adept at predicting potential fire outbreaks precursors such as unusually dry conditions or areas of high lightning strike frequencies.

In instances of detected fires, the system rapidly sends alerts to local firefighting teams. Satellite imagery plays an integral role in this scenario, enabling fire crews to visualize the area's topography, plan their attack strategies, and prioritize resource allocation.

Arguably, the biggest victory of this AI deployment is its capability to anticipate where fires might break out based on vegetative cover, weather patterns, and historical data. This means firefighting teams can strategize preemptively, arrange resources, and, more importantly, initiate preventive measures, thus solidifying AI as a steadfast ally against environmental disasters.

5.2. AI-Assisted Earthquake Response in San Francisco

Given the high Earthquake potential in the Pacific Northwest, it becomes exceedingly crucial to be equipped with a vigorous response mechanism. The Earthquake Early Detection (EED) system that harnesses real-time seismic data with AI modeling is one such effective measure in place.

Through various ground motion sensors spread across a vast area, the EED system amasses seismic data. The AI analyzes this data and offers early warning alerts in advance of an earthquake's most disruptive shock waves. While the warning time might seem extremely short (ranging from seconds to a minute), it is crucial. It allows automatic systems to halt trains, close off gas lines, stop surgeries in hospitals, thereby considerably minimizing the potential damage to both life and infrastructure.

When an earthquake occurs, EED's predictive models, enabled by machine learning algorithms, assist in estimating the damage in the aftermath. Collating existing built environment data and the quake's impact, the algorithm forecasts infrastructure damages, aiding efficient dispatch of emergency teams.

5.3. Urban Traffic Management for Emergency Situations

Our cities' ever-expanding population and commensurate congestion is another area where AI has shown remarkable resilience. During emergency situations, response times can be a crucial determinant of outcomes. AI-powered traffic management systems aim to streamline and expedite emergency services in bustling cities.

These AI systems work in tandem with existing traffic infrastructures. They integrate with real-time video feeds from traffic cameras and use machine learning algorithms to predict and analyze city-wide traffic movements. When an emergency call is registered, the AI system dynamically plans the quickest route for first responders. This routing takes into consideration an array of variables - current traffic, traffic light timings, road conditions, and even weather conditions.

Additionally, these systems also alert surrounding drivers of an approaching emergency vehicle. Smartphone alerts or digital road signs help clear the path, ensuring response times are significantly reduced. By leveraging the power of AI, urban traffic management can transform the speed and efficiency of emergency services in our bustling metropolises.

Artificial intelligence enables unprecedented efficiencies, whether it's predicting wildfires, managing after-earthquake efforts, or hastening emergency response in traffic-swelled streets. What remains a common thread in all these case studies is AI's transformative potential in harnessing data, learning, and predicting to enhance our world's emergency response preparedness and recovery. It strengthens our resolve in the face of the unexpected, bringing an element of foreseeability to inherently uncertain events. As we further refine these powerful tools, AI's potential to revolutionize emergency response only grows.

Chapter 6. Real-time Analytics in Emergency Response: Effective and Fast

Real-time analytics is in the vanguard of evolving technologies that are transforming emergency response strategies worldwide. The application of real-time analytics in emergency response scenarios is assuring faster, more efficient and effective execution of operations that protect life, property, and the environment.

6.1. The Potential of Real-Time Analytics

As the name suggests, real-time analytics involves the instantaneous processing and analysis of data as soon as it enters the database. It is a potent tool for enhancing traditional emergency response tactics that used to rely on manual data analysis, which could be time-consuming and prone to errors.

In an emergency where every second matters, real-time data analytics provides critical insights instantaneously, giving emergency responders an edge over the conventional response actions. It can predict impending hazards, provide insights into the most effective response strategies, track the progress of ongoing emergency operations, and post-event, aid in understanding how these situations unfolded for future prevention and preparedness measures.

6.2. Real-Time Analytics: Enabling Fast and Efficient Emergency Responses

Real-time analytics brings a new dimension to the processes of emergency response. It leverages powerful machine algorithms, advanced computing and data visualization tools, that provide situational awareness in real-time, enabling fast and calculated decisions.

One of the unique features of real-time analytics is its ability to analyze vast amounts of data from various sources, such as IoT devices, social media, and traditional media. For example, in the case of a wildfire, real-time analytics algorithms could consolidate data from weather stations, firefighters on the ground, the local populace, drones, and satellites. The algorithms analyze the data almost instantaneously, providing detailed insights into the wildfire's current status, direction of spread, intensity, and possible areas of propagation.

These insights allow emergency teams to position their resources strategically for effective fire suppression and evacuation operations. The real-time element is crucial because, in a wildfire situation, factors such as wind direction, temperature, and humidity can change rapidly, and updated information is essential to maintain the effectiveness of the response measures.

6.3. How AI and Machine Learning Enhance Real-Time Analytics in Emergency Response

AI and Machine Learning (ML) algorithms are instrumental in enhancing real-time analytics, enabling it to predict and analyze trends from the processed data swiftly and efficiently. These technologies leverage computational algorithms and statistical techniques to learn and predict future outcomes based on historical data patterns.

In the application to emergency response, AI models can be trained on past emergency situations to detect and predict possible situations like floods and wildfires. For instance, they can analyze data from river pressure sensors, weather patterns, and historical flood records. AI can predict potential flood hotspots, enabling emergency squads to prepare and act accordingly, mitigating the severity of the flood.

Machine learning, on the other hand, can identify relevant patterns and trends from the real-time data gathered during an emergency. For example, ML algorithms can follow social media trends during a crisis, identifying critical needs and challenges expressed by the public, and provide this information to the response teams for necessary action.

6.4. The Future: Challenges and Opportunities in Implementing Real-Time Analytics

While real-time analytics has demonstrated potential in making emergency responses more efficient, it also presents some challenges.

One of the most significant challenges lies with data: data quality, data management, and data privacy. Emergency response teams need high-quality, accurate data to make precise predictions and decisions. Also, managing real-time data from various sources necessitates robust computing infrastructures. Finally, handling sensitive data while respecting privacy regulations is a delicate balance that requires careful consideration.

Furthermore, rolling out AI and ML-powered real-time analytics systems requires sizable investments which may be daunting for resource-strapped emergency departments.

Despite these challenges, there is a growing recognition of the pivotal role real-time analytics can play in revolutionising emergency response. As the technology advances, it will progressively overcome these current hindrances. Future enhancements may include improved interfaces for emergency responders, more resilient machine learning algorithms, stringent data privacy safeguards, and more affordable high-speed computing infrastructures.

To conclude, real-time analytics already marks an epoch shift in emergency management. Leveraging the synergy of AI and machine learning, it paves the way for a future where emergency response is no more reactive but predictive, efficient, and effective.

Chapter 7. AI for Natural Disasters: Role in Prevention, Mitigation, and Recovery

A severe tornado devastates a town, a raging wildfire covers acres, or a catastrophic flood inundates neighborhoods – these are instances of common natural disasters that pose significant threats to human life, properties, and the environment. The ability to predict, respond, and recover from such disasters is critical, hence the growing reliance on artificial intelligence. AI is now undeniably at the forefront in revolutionizing the various stages of dealing with natural disasters. In this chapter, we're going to cover the key contributions AI has made in prevention, mitigation, and recovery tasks that form the backbone of disaster management operations.

7.1. Predicting Natural Disasters

Prediction is commonly the first step in the direction toward disaster resilience. AI algorithms have been in use for a considerable period of time to predict natural calamities by analyzing historical patterns and utilizing forecast models. To put it simply, they learn from previous instances, making timely predictions about possible recurrences.

Machine learning, one of AI's fundamental subsets, has been instrumental in predicting severe weather conditions. For instance, IBM's Deep Thunder project leverages machine learning methods to produce highly detailed weather forecasts. Deep Thunder crunches a large amount of data like temperature, humidity, wind velocity, and combines them with topographical data to predict precipitation amounts and locations with startling accuracy.

Flood forecasting is another area where AI shines. A team of researchers at the University of Reading has successfully used a branch of machine learning called 'Long Short Term Memory' (LSTM) to predict river water levels up to five days in advance. By harnessing the LSTM model, data on previous flow rates, rainfall levels, temperature, and humidity are analyzed, offering cities valuable time to prepare.

7.2. Mitigation Measures

If prevention isn't possible, the next step is mitigation. AI has been increasingly used to model different disaster scenarios and suggest optimal mitigation measures by creating data-backed simulations of the disaster event.

One example of AI in mitigation involves earthquake-prone areas. AI is used to generate simulations based on various factors, including the strength of the earthquake, the depth of the focus, the distance from the epicenter, etc. Based on these simulations, hazard maps are created which help identify high-risk areas and enable urban planners in devising safer building codes and land use plans.

AI is also making strides in mitigating the impacts of wildfires. A startup called Descartes Labs has developed a wildfire detection system which uses real-time satellite imagery. This system incorporates deep learning algorithms to differentiate between smoke plumes and clouds, thus informing quicker fire detection and response.

7.3. Emergency Response

When a disaster does strike, an effective and efficient response can dramatically reduce its impacts. AI assists emergency teams by making the response process smarter and faster.

AI can process vast amounts of data rapidly, identifying people and resources that need immediate attention. By analyzing social media posts or emergency calls, AI can help prioritize areas of greatest need. Moreover, utilizing drone-facilitated AI can make search-and-rescue operations more efficient, identifying survivors in difficult-to-reach places and gathering vital information about the affected areas.

7.4. Recovery and Rehabilitation

After the disaster, the focus shifts to recovery and rehabilitation. Using AI in reviewing damage and rebuilding efforts after a disaster has tremendous potential.

Post-disaster, AI can help assess the extent of damage by analyzing satellite and drone imagery. This helps in effectively distributing resources, prioritizing areas that need immediate attention, and facilitating faster insurance claims.

AI also aids in the long-term rehabilitation process. For instance, after the 2010 earthquake in Haiti, AI was used to identify temporary shelters which could be transformed into permanent homes. The AI model used satellite images to find these shelters, aiding in bringing stability and normalcy faster to the lives affected by the disaster.

7.5. Building the Future with AI

There is little doubt that AI has a profound role to play in dealing with natural disasters. Its ability to predict, mitigate, respond to, and recover from disaster situations is significantly reshaping how we approach emergency management.

The potency of AI isn't merely in its capacity to crunch numbers swiftly or to 'learn' from data patterns. More vitally, it's in the lives saved, properties protected, and the chance it gives communities to rebound quicker post-disaster. It is this power of AI that is driving researchers and innovators to keep exploring its limitless potential in transforming our battle against natural disasters. The future is indeed promising, and with a tool as potent as AI, we are better equipped than ever to face and conquer these challenges.

To put it succinctly, AI isn't an abstract, otherworldly concept in disaster management anymore. It is here, it is practical, and it is already making a difference. AI's role in disaster management is not only momentous but is bound to grow and evolve in the coming years, rendering it not just an assistant, but a game-changer in our quest for a disaster-resilient world.

Chapter 8. AI in Medical Emergencies: Faster Diagnosis, Better Prognosis

When a medical emergency strikes, time is of the essence. A delay of even a few minutes can sometimes make the difference between recovery and disability, or even life and death. AI, or artificial intelligence, is leading the fight against time, arming medical professionals with tools that allow for faster, more accurate diagnoses, better-informed treatment strategies, and improved patient outcomes.

8.1. The Power of AI in Diagnostics

A key area where AI has made significant strides is in diagnostics. Machine learning algorithms can scan medical images — such as CT scans, MRIs or X-rays — and highlight areas of concern, often with accuracy comparable to or even surpassing that of human experts.

Consider a stroke, one of the leading causes of death and disability globally. In most types of stroke, time is absolutely critical. AI software, such as that offered by companies like Viz.ai, can flag potential stroke victims in a matter of minutes, thereby drastically reducing decision-making time. These rapid response times can enable treatment to start more quickly, potentially staving off severe disability or death.

AI isn't only useful in the diagnosis of acute conditions. It also has significant potential in the diagnosis of chronic disease. Deep learning, a subset of AI, can analyze multiple layers of data – including genetics, lifestyle, and even zip codes – to predict individual susceptibility to diseases like diabetes or heart disease. This enables earlier intervention and treatment, potentially halting or slowing disease progression and improving patient prognosis.

8.2. Optimal Treatment Strategies with AI

Once clearly identified, treating medical emergencies promptly and correctly is vital in maximizing patient survival and well-being. AI can help significantly in this by determining the most effective treatment strategy for specific individuals.

For example, IBM's Watson for Oncology uses AI to assist doctors in identifying personalized, evidence-based cancer treatments. Watson takes into account a vast amount of data — from a patient's medical records and the latest medical research to data on similar cases from around the globe — to give doctors a nuanced picture of the potential benefits and risks of various treatment options.

In the case of sepsis, an AI platform known as Sepsis Watch processes real-time patient data to help identify the onset of this potentially deadly infection before it fully develops. This could enable doctors and nurses to act fast, providing treatment that could save a patient's life.

8.3. AI and Telemedicine: Bridging the Accessibility Gap

AI strategies also have the potential to reduce disparities in emergency medical treatment. Telemedicine, which uses digital technology to provide healthcare remotely, has surged in the midst of the COVID-19 pandemic, and AI is poised to enhance its effectiveness further.

Health applications equipped with AI capabilities help screen symptoms, alert individuals to potential health emergencies, and recommend when to seek medical consultation. In cases when reaching a healthcare facility is difficult, such applications can provide interim advice for managing symptoms while arrangements for appropriate medical support are made.

Moreover, AI can allow telemedicine platforms to triage patients effectively, ensuring that those requiring urgent care are attended to in a timely fashion. AI models could analyze a patient's symptoms, vital signs, or responses to certain questions and estimate the urgency of their situation. Based on these estimations, patients can be prioritized and connected to healthcare providers accordingly.

8.4. The Future of AI in Medical Emergencies

While we've seen significant advancements in AI's application to medical emergencies, the horizon remains laden with potential. As machine learning algorithms continue to learn and evolve, so too will their precision and efficacy in diagnosing and treating various health conditions.

Furthermore, as AI is widely accepted and integrated into healthcare systems, its utility in training and education will expand. Virtual reality (VR) paired with AI could create highly realistic emergency scenarios for training purposes. AI-powered VR could adapt in real-time to how a student reacts, providing unprecedented levels of interactivity and immersion, thereby shaping a more competent generation of emergency responders.

AI also offers the promise of predictive analytics. By harnessing the vast amounts of data collected by health systems, smart wearables, and even social media platforms, AI can predict when and where medical emergencies might take place with a relevant degree of accuracy. Such technology could alert individuals or healthcare systems to impending emergencies ahead of time, allowing them to take preventative measures and deploy resources more effectively.

Ultimately, AI shows tremendous promise in revolutionizing the ways we approach medical emergencies. Faster diagnosis, personalized treatment, bridging accessibility gaps, and even the promise of prediction – all depict a hopeful future where AI is an integral part of emergency medical response, bolstering our collective resilience. Every minute saved through the use of AI could result in many more lives saved, significantly enhancing our emergency preparedness and recovery efforts.

Chapter 9. Ethical Considerations: AI in Emergency Response

In the embrace of Artificial Intelligence (AI) for enhancing emergency response outcomes, it is imperative we pause for a moment to consider the ethical implications. Leveraging AI in emergency situations implicates a variety of matters spanning privacy, accuracy, bias, and responsibility. Grasping these basic concerns will catalyze the ethical deployment of AI, reinforcing trust in the technology and ensuring the best results for all.

9.1. Privacy and Data Management

AI systems thrive on data. The more data available, the more accurate and effective these systems may be. In the scenario of an emergency dispatch system powered by AI, data points such as callers' locations, medical background information, and nature of emergencies may be gathered to assist in the prediction, comprehension, and management of emergencies. However, it raises questions about privacy and how this data is managed while complying with legal guidelines.

One central question is whether organizations have the right to store personal information such as health data and for how long? In addition, who has access to this data? The use of encrypted storage and transmission protocols are essential to prevent unauthorized access and uphold data privacy. Storage duration must also comply with regulations, being kept only as long as required by law. Organizations need to tread a fine line, balancing between gathering sufficient data for AI systems to work efficiently and upholding the individual's right to privacy.

Another critical aspect of privacy revolves around consent. Do individuals know their data is being used to augment an AI system, and if so, have they explicitly consented to it? Implementing clear and informed consent procedures becomes paramount. Although these may slow immediate response times, these are crucial for ensuring trust and respect for privacy.

9.2. Accuracy and Bias

AI systems, underpinned by Machine Learning (ML), are only as effective as the data they're trained on. If the training data is skewed, biased, or of inadequate quality, the AI is likely to propagate those errors, with potentially severe consequences in emergency response situations.

Inaccurate predictions could lead to inappropriate responses, such as dispatching the wrong type of assistance or incorrectly prioritizing incidents. A biased AI could marginalize certain populations, for instance, ineffectively predicting emergencies in areas with less historical data. A critical challenge lies in training AI on comprehensive, unbiased datasets, regularly reviewing, and iterating model designs for continuous improvement.

9.3. Autonomous Decision Making

AI systems have the potential to progressively make autonomous decisions. A high-stakes field like emergency response necessitates deliberation on the extent to which we are willing to let AI make potentially life-saving determinations.

For instance, an AI system might predict a patient's likeliest diagnosis based on their symptoms or determine the best course of action for a developing emergency. But, should an AI system make the final call or should a human always be in control of such decisions? Transparency around the role AI plays in decision-making processes is crucial to preserve trust and manage expectations correctly.

9.4. Responsibility for AI Outcomes

Deciding who's accountable when an AI system makes a mistake, especially within the context of emergency response, presents a daunting dilemma. Existing legal frameworks are ill-prepared for addressing such scenarios.

Is the software developer who engineered the AI code accountable? Or the emergency response team that deployed it? Clear guidelines need to be crafted delineating responsibility and accountability in case of an unfavorable outcome.

9.5. Inclusion and Accessibility

It is vital to ensure that AI-powered emergency response services are accessible and inclusive to all populations, irrespective of their language proficiency, tech savviness, or physical abilities. For instance, voice-recognition AI systems need to comprehend diverse accents and dialects.

To summarize, the integration of AI in emergency response presents immense potential, but it also ushers in a host of complex ethical questions that must be accounted for. A thorough understanding of AI, transparency about its utilization, inclusion of diverse perspectives, and the formulation of robust ethical guidelines are crucial to navigate this intricate landscape. Only then can we fully harness the power of AI, ensuring we leverage this revolutionary technology to save lives, safeguard property, and protect our environment more efficiently.

Chapter 10. Challenges & Roadblocks in AI-Assisted Emergency Management

Certainly, AI-enabled emergency management is poised to transform the way we respond to crises. However, like with any technology, its application in emergency management is not without its challenges and roadblocks. Let's explore these in depth, taking into account the various aspects involved.

10.1. Technical Challenges

Understanding the complexity of emergencies and disaster situations is an essential task for AI systems. A lack of standardization influences the design, training, and implementation of these systems to a large extent. A model flawlessly trained and tested in one region might falter when applied to another due to unique, local characteristics.

Ensuring real reliability is another challenge. AI systems need to process vast amounts of data and make real-time decisions. Even slight miscalculations could lead to missed emergency alerts or give rise to false positives, both potentially having serious repercussions.

Interoperability between various AI systems is another stumbling block. AI projects in emergency management, often designed and built in isolation, struggle to communicate and collaborate effectively with each other, leading to less than optimal outcomes.

10.2. Data Chenges

Data-related obstacles are manifold. The accuracy and reliability of

AI forecasts heavily depend on the quality and quantity of data available. Finding high-quality, relevant, and diverse datasets for training purposes can be difficult, especially for rare but high-consequence emergency events like earthquakes or terrorist attacks.

Issues of privacy and consent emerge, too, especially when AI systems are trained on sensitive data. Balancing the need to use personal data for better emergency response with the equally important need to respect privacy proves challenging.

10.3. Ethical Challenges

AI systems are only as equitable as the data they're trained on. Bias in AI—stemming from biased training data or inherent model bias—has serious implications, potentially leading to discriminatory outcomes in emergencies, when stakes are highest. Ensuring fairness across different demographics during the response can be a difficult yet important objective.

There's also the black-box problem. The complex algorithms of AI, particularly in deep learning models, can be difficult to understand and interpret. In high-stake situations such as emergencies, not comprehending why a certain decision was made can be risky.

10.4. Legislative Challenges

Legislative and regulatory issues pose yet another challenge for AI in emergency response. AI systems are relatively novel. As such, many jurisdictions lack appropriate guidelines or regulatory frameworks to govern their use in emergency management. This prompts risk of misuse or abuse and could lead to litigations, hampering response efforts.

10.5. Deployment and Acceptance Challenges

Deployment of AI technologies on the ground isn't always smooth. Infrastructure compatibility, technical glitches, and system incompatibilities are usual hurdles to implementation.

Moreover, for AI systems to aid effectively in emergency management, they must be accepted by both the responders and the public. Fears and misconceptions about AI, or a lack of understanding of its benefits, could impede user trust and adoption, hindering the technology's potential in emergency management.

In conclusion, while AI carries immense potential for enhancing emergency preparedness and response, it is crucial to responsibly navigate these challenges. With a nuanced understanding, cooperative efforts, and regulatory interventions, we can ensure that the power of AI is harnessed to save lives and mitigate the impacts of emergencies effectively, ethically, and fairly. The journey is complex, but the rewards promise to be significant.

Chapter 11. The Future: Evolving Role of AI in Emergency Response

Artificial intelligence (AI) plays an increasingly essential role in emergency response and disaster management. Its growing influence goes beyond mere integration into existing systems; it is becoming a core component of advanced, evolving strategies. AI's intense data-crunching capabilities, paired with the sophistication of its predictive models, enhance the efficiency, readiness, and recovery capacities of emergency interventions.

11.1. AI's Role in Prediction and Early Warning

Prediction and early warning form the bedrock of disaster management. AI stands at the forefront of these tasks, enabling the creation of models that can anticipate disasters by analyzing extensive data from different sources. It uses machine learning algorithms to learn from both historical and real-time datasets, drawing relationships between variables that would seem unrelated to the human eye. Such predictive models can give accurate predictions about the likelihood of disasters, the most affected areas, and the scale of potential damage.

Use of AI in predicting natural disasters is already visible today. For example, Google's flood forecasting initiative uses AI to predict flood possibilities. The technology uses a combination of elevation maps and telemetry data from thousands of government monitoring stations. When integrated with weather forecasts, it creates highly accurate flood predictions. This use of AI in early warnings saves lives and reduces property damage.

11.2. AI Enhancing Emergency Preparedness

Another aspect where AI shines brightly is enhancing emergency preparedness. For instance, it can help plan escape routes or evacuation plans. AI algorithms can use traffic data, the physical maps of the city, and forecasts about disaster impact to outline the safest and quickest route for evacuation. These routes can continually update based on real-time data, making them more efficient and adaptive.

AI also aids in resource allocation during emergencies. With AI, authorities can understand where to stock essential supplies for the fastest delivery during a crisis. Deep learning algorithms address population density, location accessibility, local infrastructure, and resources to create allocation models that are highly efficient.

11.3. AI in Disaster Response

When disaster strikes, AI keeps stepping up the game—it assists in coordinating an effective response. By using images and data from satellites, drones, and ground-based sensors, AI can assess the damage. The damage assessment is crucial for designing an efficient response strategy.

Humanitarian organizations, such as the Red Cross, are employing AI to evaluate the extent of damage from natural disasters. They use satellite images fed into a machine-learning algorithm trained to identify damages. This method allows these organizations to understand the scale of the disaster quickly and allocate their resources accordingly.

Additionally, AI can support search and rescue missions by using drone footage to locate survivors. During the 2015 Nepal earthquake, AI played a key role in analyzing drone images, helping to find survivors among millions of square feet of rubble.

11.4. AI in Disaster Recovery

Post disaster, AI greatly aids in quantifying losses and streamlining the recovery process. Insurers have already started using AI to accurately evaluate insurance claims post-disasters. AI can also aid rebuilding efforts by predicting which areas need help first and providing comprehensive data on the type and extent of the damages.

AI also plays an integral role in ensuring effective communication during and after disasters. Social media platforms use AI algorithms to surface emergency content, providing real-time updates and ensuring important information reaches everyone affected.

11.5. Limitations and Ethical Considerations of AI in Emergency Response

While AI has been influential in emergency response, it does come with its own set of limitations and ethical issues. Issues like AI bias, data privacy, and reliance on technology raise concerns. AI bias can occur when the AI system's training data is not representative, resulting in inaccurate predictions. Data privacy continues to loom larger, particularly when AI uses personal data for prediction or disaster management.

Moreover, the increasing reliance on AI technology questions the human role in disaster management. AI should work as an aid to human intelligence rather than a replacement. Recognition of these limitations is critical for determining future strategies ensuring that human judgment and ethical considerations aren't lost.

In conclusion, AI's role in emergency response is undoubtedly expansive and continuously evolving. Its potential seems limitless when it comes to enhancing prediction, facilitating preparedness, coordinating disaster response, or aiding recovery. That said, it's essential to navigate the limitations and ethical considerations of AI use. As we proceed into the next level of technological advancements, AI's role in emergency response will only grow more essential, sophisticated, and efficient. The future of AI in emergency management is shining bright, promising safer and better-prepared communities.